THE GREEN

The village almost certainly grew up around The Green, which was originally surrounded by wc
more it has been at the confluence of what we now call Church Hill, Wades Hill, Station Road
hundred years ago these were little more than country lanes.
There used to be an open well on the Lower Green but about 1850, after a child fell in and drc
replaced by a pump. This stood just to the west of the small tree lined pond shown at 521 on
was also a small pond on the Upper Green at this time, but it was filled in before the 1895 survey.)

Around 1883 piped water was laid on to the village and the pump fell into disuse. Over the next two decades the pump and
pond were replaced by a fountain, set in a garden bounded by railings. At the same time shops sprung up to turn The Green
into a shopping centre.

The fountain and garden disappeared about the time of the Second World War, as did the last vestiges of the old village
atmosphere (so I have been told). By then, of course, Winchmore Hill was very much the residential suburb of London we
know today. But even in modern times the Lower Green plays annual host to a Maypole, as well as a Christmas Tree, in an
attempt to capture the spirit of the old village.

1865 Ordnance Survey Map round The Green: Thanks to the Ordnance Survey and the Southgate Civic Trust for
permission to reproduce the section of map shown on the next page (not to original scale).

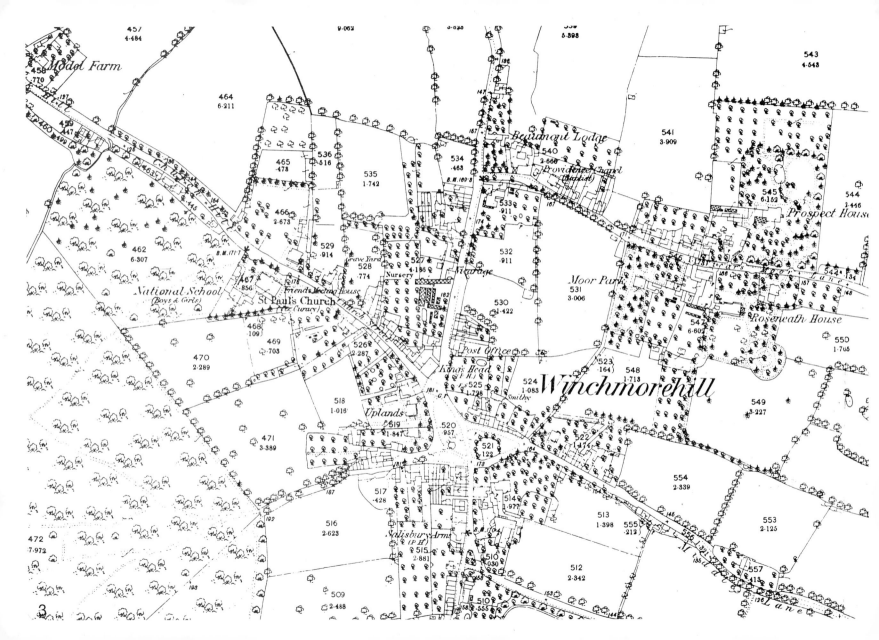

16, The Green; The Bowens ran the florists "Elizabeth of the Green" for 25 years until their retirement to Norfolk in July 2000. They kindly let me take this snap of the rear to their premises in April 1990. At first sight the view seems quite unexceptional but the dark material is clapperboard, as found in the cottages at the base of Church Hill and top of Wades Hill. This helps point a clue to the age of the property.

   I have spoken to the Bowens and David Hicks, who runs the adjoining "Winchmore Antiques" at No14, a number of times. The following comes from my conversations with them and from "Enfield: Portrait of a London Borough" by Matthew Eccleston - who had also spoken to them.

The rear sections of numbers 14 and 16 The Green were almost certainly built in the late 18th century as one residential property at ground and first floor level (though parts of No16 may even date back to the 16th century). The front to the house was, however, about eight feet back from the current frontage. When No16 was a florist, the old front line was marked by a conspicuous change of floor level and the original door and staircase were to the right (when viewed from the street).

   By the time of the Edmonton Enclosure Award Map of 1801 the original house had been divided into two, the partition wall being softwood veneer. A front door to No14 would have been added at the time of the partition and it is thought that the extra level and staircase to "Winchmore Antiques" would also have been constructed then.

The two cottages are shown with their front gardens in the OS Map of 1865 at page 3. However, by the time of the 1895 survey the current frontages had been added - possibly between 1884 and 1891.

For over a century now, Nos14 and 16 have been used for commercial purposes, but parts date back to a rural residential past.

The Green looking towards "The King's Head".

This photograph was kindly given to me by the late Mr. H.K.Surtees and is reproduced with his consent.

I have been able to match up the shops shown with the 1903-4 Kelly's Street Directory as follows, starting to the west: George Nix's Dairy; Dunnett's Tailors; Mrs M.Williams's Confectioners; C. Palmer's Hairdressers; W.Gabriel - corn and seed merchants; F.G Barker - Ironmonger; J. Garrard and Sons - Builders. To help give the reader modern terms of reference, Gabriel's was "Elizabeth of the Green" and Barker's was where "Winchmore Antiques" now is. When this snap was taken the shops round The Green served most, if not all, of the village's needs.

"The King's Head," Winchmore Hill, in 1860. Sketch by Dr. Cresswell: Reproduced courtesy of the "Enfield Gazette."

"The King's Head" has probably existed in some form on this site since at least 1700. Horace Regnart describes the inn as, "an old, brown brick, two storied building with a porch with imitation marble pillars. In front was a low wooden fence on which they often used to put out the metal beer tankards. On the left of the porch was a fine wistaria. The proprietor was Ballantine." The main entrance described cannot actually be seen in this sketch as it was further along Wades Hill.

In 1860 the pub's beer garden was on the opposite corner of Wades Hill and is at 525 on the 1865 OS Map at page 3. Miss Cresswell said the garden was "where lavender and rosemary and white pinks flourished, and where there was a pond, on which floated waxen water lilies...."

In 1879 - 80 the existing premises, used for many years as a Post Office, were built on the S.E corner of Wades Hill - where the perimeter fence to the beer garden can be seen on the right. The "King's Head" itself was rebuilt in the late 1890's to give us the elegant structure that overlooks The Green today.

CHURCH HILL

In the first half of the 13th century The Holy Trinity Priory, at Aldgate in the City of London, purchased land in the field known as Yarildesfeld, which lay in the angle between Church Hill and Wades Hill, near to The Green. At that time it appears to have abutted what became known as Enfield Chase.

The Victoria County History's reconstruction of the area for 1600AD indicates that by then Church Hill was known as Highwood Lane and it led to Highwood Gate to the Chase, situated approximately where "The Winchmore Arms" now stands. A privately owned wood bordered the lane to its SW.

The 1801/2 Edmonton Enclosure Award refers to Church Hill as Winchmore Hill Lane. In 1826 - 7 St Paul's Chapel-of-Ease was erected on land donated by Walker Gray. At that time the lane was known as Chase Hill. In 1851 the Chapel-of-Ease was elevated to the status of Church and by the time of the 1865 OS Map (page 3), the lane had three names! The SE section (ie. nearest The Green) was Church Street, the NW segment Cock Hill and the middle part Church Hill.

By the time of the 1895 survey, the NW section (ie. towards "The Winchmore Arms") was called Winchmore Hill Road and the remainder Church Hill. The 1899 - 1900 Kelly's Street Directory calls the whole stretch Winchmore Hill Road, but in the 1902 - 3 edition this was reversed and the whole road was called Church Hill - and remains thus today.

Devon House: I am grateful to Mr D. Kent of current occupants Edwards Estates for the photograph, dated 18th April 1933. About ten years ago he was also good enough to give me a guided tour of the premises and supply me with the results of his research, upon which much of the following is based. Architectural evidence seems to point to an origin date somewhere between 1708 and 1730, though the sash windows are probably Victorian replacement features.

The Edmonton Enclosure awards of 1801 list a William Fox as owner of the plot of land upon which Devon House and "The King's Head" were built. By 1825 three small cottages bridged the gap between the two and these survived until 1896 when "The King's Head" was rebuilt and a fire station put in their place.

For most of the second half of the 19th century the House was occupied by the Langley family, who were butchers. A series of butchers followed them early in the 20th century - T.Gocher then W. Potter then William Phillips. The remains of the old slaughter house can still be seen in the yard.

Devon House was listed as a Grade 2 building in 1950. It deteriorated badly in the mid 1980's but was tastefully refurbished by Edwards Estates a few years later.

St. Paul's Vicarage; In the middle of the 19th century Glenwood House was used as St. Paul's Vicarage. Later on, Rose Cottage in Vicars Moor Lane fulfilled this function. However, in 1913 estimates totalling £2,587 were accepted and the present structure was built on land given by the benevolent William Paulin.

This view is from near the Denleigh Gardens entrance and is by courtesy of the "Enfield Gazette". Judging from the dress and immature trees it was probably taken not long after the Vicarage opened.

St. Paul's Church Interior: This photograph was supplied by the late H.K. Surtees with agreement to publish. It is from a set of local views that probably date back about a hundred years.

We tend to think of crime against church property as being of modern derivation, but Miss Cresswell tells us, "Winchmore Hill Church was consecrated by Bishop Howley in 1828. In 1844 some thieves broke in to steal the Altar Cloths and Communion Plate, but fortunately the Silver had been removed to the Curate's house. They accidentally set fire to the Church, and the east end was much damaged. Mrs. Todd, of Uplands, gave the carved Altar, Pulpit, and Reading Desks, that there might be no 'hangings' to be stolen."

Woodside Cottages: This lovely undated shot looks NW down Church Hill past "Woodside Cottages," which still exist today. One of these clapperboard cottages bears an inscription that indicates it was built about 1785 and was used as the old village school, though it was superseded in this function when a new school was built adjoining St. Paul's Church in 1859.

WINCHMORE HILL ROAD

This is another before and after scenario thanks, again, to the archives of the "Enfield Gazette." The first photo is labelled "By Hope House and Home Farm about 1930", whilst the second is a comparison shot a few years later. The nearest house to the viewer is No156. Tintern Gardens is opposite Nos 146 - 148 downview.

Francis Russell's 1776 Map, used for the division of Enfield Chase soon after, shows a lane following the line of the modern road along a boundary of the Chase. (Winchmore Hill Gate is at its junction with what we call Church Hill.) The 1801 - 2 Edmonton Enclosure Award Map shows the name as Chase Side Road. This is also the name shown on the sketch plan accompanying the sale catalogue for Grovelands (then 'The Grove') in 1834.

The lane does not seem to bear a name in the 1865 OS Map but Hope House is marked on the southern side about a third of the way towards Southgate from the base of Cock Hill (now Church Hill). By the time of the 1895 survey it is clearly shown as Winchmore Hill Road and Home Farm is marked by Houndsden Gutter, a few hundred feet north west of Hope House.

Perversely, in the 1899 - 1900 Kelly's Street Directory Church Hill is called Winchmore Hill Road, whilst this road is named Chase Side. The situation is resolved in the Kelly's for 1902 - 3, Chase Side assuming the title of Winchmore Hill Road for good.

The 1899 - 1900 Kelly's shows Joe King as occupying the 62 acre Home Farm, which at the time was part of the massive estate owned by the Taylor family. It was sold in their 1902 sales for £8,400. Mr King was still listed as the occupant in the 1909 - 10 Kelly's.

Hope House was also part of the Taylors' estates but was not sold at this time, presumably being sold off about 1930 when the family was living in Oxfordshire. It was probably a late 18th century farmhouse that pre - dated Grovelands Mansion and had been turned into a dower house by the Taylors. (A dower house is a portion of a couple's estate given over to the wife's use.)

Eva Aldridge, nee Baker, featured in my "Winchmore Hill Lives". She was born in 1903 and said of Hope House, "At first, like the other children of my age, I used to call this the 'haunted house', but I came to realise that a hermit lived there. Apparently he had lost all his family and this had so affected him that he never went out other than to collect the shopping which was delivered to his door."

EVERSLEY PARK ROAD

The Victoria County History for Middlesex states that a Highgate Street of c1255 may be a forerunner of this road. It says that a Highgate Lane of c1330 might also be so. The Edmonton Enclosure Award Map for 1801 - 2 shows an unnamed track following a line similar to that of the modern road.

In her "Memories of a Lost Village," Henrietta Cresswell describes the "road" as it was when out walking with her brother on a fine April's day in about 1860, "The hills between the Tavern (now "The Winchmore Arms"), and the fields on which Chaseville Park was afterwards built, were so steep that the valley resembled a half -opened book with the swiftly running streamlet in the fold of the binding. There were old houses, or rather cottages, all down one side of the road, and two or three more important dwellings on the opposite hillside. There was a mineral well here, so strongly impregnated with Epsom salts, that in the early part of the last (19th) century it nearly led to Winchmore Hill becoming a fashionable Spa...... As the ground rose, all houses were left behind, and at the summit, a ragged barn and a field gate marked the entrance to a cart road leading to Oak Lodge, half a mile away, and a fine view was obtained towards Slades Hill and South Lodge...... Before the houses of Chaseville Park or the great mansion of Eversley were thought of, much less built, the lane was a complete avenue of beeches and oaks meeting overhead, wide stretches of grass were on either side, deep ditches overgrown with brambles and dog rose bushes, rushes three feet long might be gathered for basket plaiting, and now and again squirrels might be seen running in a spiral course up some smooth beech trunk, or a weasel gliding snakelike across the road."

At this time the road was known as Cock Hill from an old gallows or gibbet that stood in the vicinity, probably near "The Winchmore Arms" (so long known as "The Chaseside Tavern"). Alan Dumayne writes, ".....it took me some time to follow the reasoning . For gallows, read gallus which is an old English form of the word gallows, and is also Latin for cock."
In 1865, only a few years after this walk, Eversley Park Estate, with its mansion, filled the NE corner side of the road. Part of the old Estate wall survives at Eversley Mount.

The 1899 - 1900 Kelly's Directory refers to the road in two parts. The southern part is still Cock Hill but the northern section is called Chase Ville Park. However, within a few years the whole road was known as Eversley Park Road, the name clearly deriving from the then adjoining Estate.

The first old view, courtesy of the Everett sisters, looks SW from about the junction with Chaseville Park Road. The second is postmarked 28th August 1951 and reflects a still rural flavour in comparatively modern times.

HIGHLANDS VILLAGE

THE NORTHERN HOSPITAL.

Highlands Village has grown up in recent years on the site of Highlands Hospital. Some of the old hospital buildings have been adapted for residential use alongside modern flats and houses. Highlands Hospital was actually two distinct Victorian establishments that eventually merged. The hospital was a centre of excellence for the treatment of "Sleeping Sickness," which led Robert De Niro to visit it when researching his role in the 1990 film "Awakenings."

The Northern Hospital: This photograph was kindly given to me in a batch by the late H.K. Surtees, all being reproduced with his permission. I believe they are from Edwardian times, though many readers will quickly recognize this building, as it still stands outwardly unchanged.

In January 1884, the Metropolitan Asylums Board purchased about 35 acres of land along the western edge of Worlds End Lane. On this site they built a 19 pavilion convalescent fever hospital of over 800 beds where children from north London hospitals could be taken after the acute stage of illness had passed, to recover in what was then the fresh country air. The Northern Hospital opened in September 1887 with its buildings arranged in a pear shape, the apex of which was near to where the photo' was taken. It was surrounded by a high brick wall and was locally known as the "Pesthouse," reflecting the fever nature. Patients were brought there twice weekly by horse ambulance from the north London hospitals.

As general health improved in London the need for fever convalescence decreased, and in February 1913, 200 beds (4 pavilions) were allocated for the treatment of tuberculosis (TB), with the addition of 62 beds by 1920.

In the early 1920s came a pandemic of Encephalitis Lethargica, covered in another caption. By the 1930s the Northern was mainly given over to caring for the after affects of that illness and TB. During the Second World War it also served as an emergency hospital, taking patients twice weekly from the bomb casualties of the East End.

On 5th July 1948 with the setting up of the National Health Service, the hospital's name was changed to Highlands and its role was that of district General Hospital for Southgate and Winchmore Hill, boasting its own casualty department in due course. Under a further reorganisation, this hospital merged with the adjoining South Lodge on 1st April 1968 as the combined new Highlands Hospital with over 600 beds. It functioned mainly as a District General Hospital serving the local community in the then recently created L.B. Enfield.

Enfield Isolation Hospital : Another old photograph courtesy of the late H.K Surtees, some of you will remember this as the former Admin. Block at Highlands. It was due to be preserved under the terms of development of Highlands Village but suffered a mysterious blaze in March 1997, being demolished by Country and Metropolitan soon afterwards.

The Enfield and Edmonton Isolation Hospital was established on a 25 acre site in 1891, administered by the Enfield and Edmonton Joint Hospital Board. It was built just north of the Northern Hospital, being separated by a brick wall, and originally had only wooden huts. However, the first brick wards appeared in 1899.

Over the decades the need for isolation wards declined and during the Second World War it accepted emergency non-infectious cases. Gradually it became a General Hospital and in 1948, with the establishment of the NHS, the name was changed to South Lodge Hospital. On 1st April 1968 it merged with the former Northern Hospital to become Highlands Hospital.

16

Ward 24 Highlands Hospital : This photograph was taken on 25th March 1995 only a few months after it was closed and its female Care of the Elderly patients moved to the new Highlands Wing at Chase Farm. My wife Yasmin, who worked on it for some years, was therefore one of the last to nurse at the hospital. The building was   subsequently demolished.

After the Great War there had been a pandemic of Encephalitis Lethargica which left patients with a baffling array of symptoms, colloquially known as "Sleeping Sickness." In November 1925 one hundred beds were allocated at the Northern Hospital to cater for children and adolescents with this problem. So expert did the hospital become that soon adult and adolescent cases for the whole of London were being referred to it, and by the late 1930s it housed over 300 afflicted persons. This "Sleeping Sickness" was a long - term condition and many cases remained when South Lodge merged into Highlands in 1968. Several of the patients were cared for on Ward 24 (once of South Lodge) and it is interesting to note that the hospital still had 20 cases on its books as late as April 1983.

Highlands Hospital 1925 : These photographs are kind courtesy of Gwen Webb, who is a member of the locally renowned Hemington family.

Unfortunately Mrs Webb was unable to supply much detail about the photos other than that they are of Highlands in 1925, though which part(s) is not clear. Presumably all the ladies shown are nurses in old style uniforms. The one with the four women by the swing shows the following names at the back, though not in any order that helps individually identify those posing - May Let (Letts); Betty Stokes, Waltham Abbey; Aunt Lou Green, nee Prince; 'Mum' Edith Ray Bennett, nee Ski; Betsy Stokes. I make that five names, so perhaps Betty and Betsy Stokes are one and the same person. Can any reader shed more light on these photographs?!

GREEN DRAGON LANE

Green Dragon Lane may have existed under the name Park Street as early as the mid 14th century, though possibly this would have been its eastern extremity. The Enfield Tithe Map of 1754 shows it as being called Filcaps Lane. This would reflect its proximity to Filcaps Gate to Enfield Chase, which was situated in the vicinity of where the modern Landra Gardens enters the main road. Cary's 1789 map of Middlesex portrays the name of Chace Lane, clearly owing to the nearness of the Chase.

The Edmonton Enclosure Award of 1801/2 refers to it as Old Park Road, Enfield Old Park being to its immediate north. Under the terms of the Enclosure Act of 1800 there was an agreement with the owner of Old Park that the road be extended west of Filcap Gate to what is now Worlds End Lane, the owner being obliged to pay Edmonton parish £5 per annum for maintenance thereafter.

I have seen an early 19th century map of the locality which shows the road as Dogkennel Lane, which is what Miss Cresswell tells us the villagers called it in the mid 19th century in her "Memories of a Lost Village."

The 1895 map shows the thoroughfare as Green Dragon Lane and this comes from "The Green Dragon " inn, now by Vicars Moor Lane but once on Green Lanes by its junction with Green Dragon Lane.

Early in the 20th century, around the time Grange Park was being built up just to the north, the stretch near Green Lanes was temporarily referred to as Grange Drive.

Eversley Park Mansion : These two photographs of Eversley Park Mansion are by kind courtesy of L.B Enfield Libraries.

The mansion was in the crook of the join between Green Dragon Lane and Eversley Park Road, sitting in grounds of 36 acres. A section of the boundary wall survives at Eversley Mount whilst the house at the corner of Green Dragon Lane, Eversley Crescent and Wades Hill was once a lodge.

The Edmonton Enclosure Map of 1801 shows most of this land belonging to a Henry Thompson. Miss Cresswell tells us the area was given over to a gravel pit and rabbit warrens at the time of her childhood in the mid 19th century.

By the mid 1860s the land was in the hands of Henry Wigan and in 1865 he had the mansion built by Cubitt for £50,000. He also sank a well to 360 feet through the London Clay, Chalk and Gault Clay to tap drinking water in the Upper Greensand. He and his wife left in 1884 and after a few years Caroline, Marchioness of Ely, took up residency. She died in 1917 and in 1921 the Wigans put the estate up for sale via Westoby's. The current high quality housing stock was then erected.

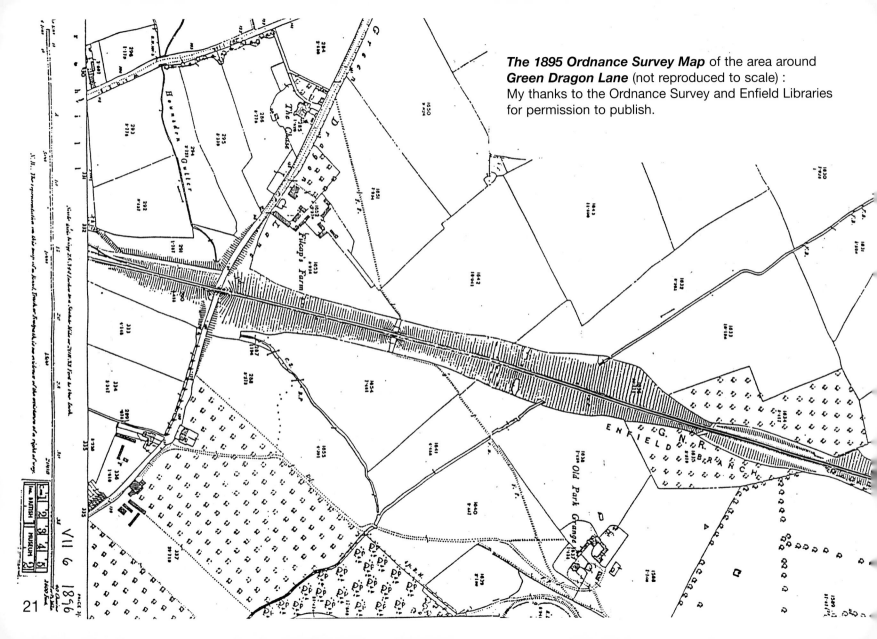

The 1895 Ordnance Survey Map of the area around **Green Dragon Lane** (not reproduced to scale) :
My thanks to the Ordnance Survey and Enfield Libraries for permission to publish.

The book's front cover - The Chase : This undated postcard captures the agricultural nature of much of the area a century ago. Reference to the 1895 Ordnance Survey Map at page 21 indicates the location of the farm in the angle between Wades Hill and Green Dragon Lane. Until the Edmonton Enclosure Act 1800 this farmland was a part of Enfield Chase - thus explaining the name.

According to Miss Cresswell, in the middle of the 19th century the farmhouse was actually a composite of a row of low, white cottages. At the end of that century the Kelly's Street Directory indicates occupancy by Edward Harry Sewell.

The last owner of The Chase was James Harvey, who purchased it in 1952 from a children's charity. He describes the residence, set in 3 acres, as being of brick with sash windows. He says there were about 19 rooms, mainly large, though the servants' quarters in the attic were dingy. In the grounds there were remnants of the rural past in the form of stables, an old brick cattle shed, two derelict greenhouses, numerous fruit trees, a kitchen garden, a rose garden and the remains of a bird aviary or chicken run.

Mr Harvey renovated the building with the help of Ewan Lewis and sold the estate in 1954, whence it was developed for housing.

Hadley Way : I am indebted to the "Enfield Gazette" for this pair of photos. I am not certain when they were taken but I believe the first would be about 1928 and the second, from the corner of Houndsden Road, around four years later.

A Bit of Old Green Dragon Lane: I am most grateful to the "Enfield Gazette" for allowing me to reproduce this lovely old sketch by the village doctor from sometime between 1865 - 70.

The accompanying article stated that the view was sketched from a point about 150 yards west of what is now Green Moor Link looking towards Green Lanes. The "house" on the right hand side is "The Retreat Inn," owned at the time by a man named Pomfret, and in the foreground is a shed which he used as a pigsty.

The old inn stood on the north - east junction of the ancient Hagfields footpath where it met Green Dragon Lane. The path was reputed to be haunted, and led down to Vicars Moor Lane along a line similar to that of the modern Green Moor Link. In her "Memories of a Lost Village," Dr Cresswell's daughter tells us that the pub was "hardly more than a beershop, where the market garden labourers went for their eleven o' clock and four o' clock (breaks)."

By the time of the 1895 OS Map, the "beershop" had been replaced by up to three houses, one of which was occupied by the Dale family.

Pike's Farm: I have two copies of this postcard, the earlier postmark being November 24th 1905.

Horace Regnart writing of late Victorian times says, on the right hand side of Green Dragon Lane starting from the eastern end, "......was Pike's Farm which extended as far as the railway line. Salmon's Brook ran through the farm roughly parallel with the road and went under Bush Hill and the New River ....Mr Pike went in extensively for fruit growing and most of the land between the road and the brook was orchards. Across the brook were grass fields with the farm buildings on the top of the hill. Opposite Hagfields path was a path across the farm. You went first downhill through orchards. You then crossed the brook by a wooden bridge and then went through the grass fields...." The path approximates to the line of modern day Old Park Ridings. Alan Dumayne estimates that the farmhouse stood just south of the junction with the Chine. Pike's Farm was thus called after the last tenant, Franklin Pike, who vacated it in 1904. It was also known as Old Park Grange and this is how it was marked on the 1895 OS Map (Pg21). It was believed to be centuries old and was owned by Lord Currie. Upon his death in 1906 it was sold to Richard Metherell, who developed the aptly named suburb of Grange Park.

Pikes Farm, Winchmore Hill.

FIRS LANE

The Victoria County History of Middlesex in its reconstruction of the area c1600 indicates that a lane had been established by then.

Horace Regnart, in his "Memories of Winchmore Hill," tells us that in late Victorian times there were just two farms and a few cottages between Hedge Lane and The New River Bridge at its northern end.

The 1936 Kelly's Directory indicates a considerable number of houses on either side, but in "Winchmore Hill Lives" Mrs B. Turner says, "In the 1920s and 1930s much of Firs Lane was bounded by farmland," whilst in his "Fond Memories of Winchmore Hill" the late Alan Dumayne (born 1929) reported, "There is a stretch of Firs Lane to the north of Barrowell Green, about 350 yards long, that is quite unique. Right through my boyhood and the wartime years, it remained a quiet country lane. It was one of the last vestiges of countryside to survive in our midst, and it was the most reluctant to change or yield to urbanisation."

Even today with its football and cricket pitches along the sides in various parts there are still green reminders of a rural past.

Gibraltar Cottages: This card bears a postmark of 24th December 1906. It is looking up Green Lanes to Gibraltar Cottages at the corner of Firs Lane, which now bears the telephone exchange which replaced them in 1937. There are two theories as to the origins of Gibraltar Cottages.

The first line of thinking is that they were built in the first twenty years of the 18th century, either after the British and Dutch captured Gibraltar in 1704 or after its permanent cessation to Great Britain by the Treaty of Utrecht in 1713. The wood screws used were apparently consistent with constructions of this era.

The other proposition is that they were built in the 1780s by local landowner John Blackburn. He was the contractor who supplied provisions to the British garrison, which successfully withstood the siege from the combined French and Spanish forces in 1779 - 83.

It is said that the corner cottage was at one time used as a post office, one wall having housed a posting box. The trees to the right of the picture, behind the fence in Firs Lane, were in over two acres of land known as Tile Barrow Field at the time of the Edmonton Enclosure Act 1800. About half of this was a pit of clay, from which presumably tiles were at one time made.

Firs Hall 1960: My thanks to Beale's Group, who owned the hall, and its long serving manger John Thorpe, for this photograph. The Hall was built just before the Great War for a man named Greenfield and it was used for dances known as "one shilling hops." By the mid 1930s the Hall was in the hands of Express Dairy. Beale's of Holloway Road made a bid for it then, but were unsuccessful. However, they obtained the right of first refusal should Express Dairy change their mind and obtained the premises (including car park) for £31,000 in 1960. The Conference and Banqueting Centre was host to thousands of wedding receptions (including my own), numerous big name entertainers (including Sir Cliff Richard) and prominent politicians (including Lady Thatcher). It was sad to see the Hall go, late in 2000.

Firs Farm: My thanks to Mr J. Waring for supplying and allowing me to publish this picture, looking north up Firs Lane. I have seen a copy of a postcard with this photograph bearing a franking of 22nd September 1911.

The farm building was not far south of the junction with Barrowell Green, though situated on the Edmonton side of Firs Lane. Alan Dumayne tells us that the building is thought to date from about 1720 and to have been constructed for Mrs Childs on land owned by the Dean and Chapter of St. Paul's.

The farm buildings appear to be marked on the Edmonton Enclosure Award Map just to the north of the extensive tracts owned by Sir James Winter Lake. A hundred years on from then the farm was tenanted by the well known Bunce family. However they vacated it in the early 1920s and the building was demolished in 1927. Part of the farm was used for housing but, unusually for our area, a large expanse was given over to playing fields, which exist to the present time.

In my 1991 book "Winchmore Hill Lives" Mrs B. Turner says, "During the (last) war the buildings by Firs Park Farm playing fields along Firs Lane were used as barracks. The soldiers were associated with an Anti - Aircraft battery near it on the fields. After the war the guns were taken down and P.O.Ws were stationed in the barracks. They farmed the fields in the vicinity and built up Farndale Avenue , which I moved to in June 1947. About that time, the Germans were repatriated and the barracks were then used to house Polish refugees for a time."

The Firs 1799: This sketch (by Miss H. E. Ewing, based on the 1799 original by Rev. Dawson Warren) is reproduced by kind courtesy of the L.B. Enfield Libraries. The mansion nestled in grounds of about 40 acres and was set back from the western side of Firs Lane approximately half way between Barrowell Green and Hedge Lane. It is said that from Hedge Lane to the drive to The Firs mansion the lane was lined by Scots Pine (pinus sylvestris). These were commonly, but incorrectly, known as Scotch Firs and so, it is thought, this avenue of trees gave both the mansion and the lane their names.

In 1799 the mansion was occupied by Sir James Winter Lake, and he owned large amounts of the surrounding land. He held senior positions with the Hudson Bay Company and it established a foothold in Alberta, Canada that eventually gave rise to the city of Edmonton. (It will be recalled that Winchmore Hill and surrounds were at this time in the parish of Edmonton). Sir James died in 1807, aged 63, and the mansion is believed to have been demolished soon after.

HEDGE LANE

Hedge Lane is indicated, and so named, in a map of the area for c1600 in the Victoria County History of Middlesex. In the 1912 Ordnance Survey Map the northern side of the road is shown as being undeveloped, with only a few buildings present. One of these is Huxley's Farm, which was sold off around 1931, whence housing was developed.

The two photographs here are by kind permission of the "Enfield Gazette." The first shows a portion of a rural looking Hedge Lane about 1930. The second is undated and shows what appears to be the same stretch at a later stage, from a slightly different angle. These houses are still there, on the northern side of the road opposite Huxley Place.

THE BOURNE/BOURNE HILL

The Victoria County History of Middlesex indicates that in about 1600 The Bourne existed as Wapull Borne and Bourne Hill as Sandpitt Lane. By the time of the 1865 Ordnance Survey, the road above (west of) The Pound was known as Bournehill, but the section below Fox Lane was titled Dog and Duck Lane. However, Miss Creswell tells us that at this time the villagers often referred to the lower stretch as "The Bone." The 1895 Survey still shows Bournehill and Dog and Duck Lane. In due course the latter became known as Bourne Hill and the former as The Bourne.

On the front page of "The Recorder for Palmers Green, Winchmore Hill and Southgate" for November 24th 1910 was an article entitled "Beauties of Bourne Hill" from which the following is an extract,
"Of all the leafy lanes and pleasant by-ways of north-east Middlesex there is none so beautiful as Bourne Hill...... There is not a bend or turn in the road that fails to offer a subject for sketch or photograph.....But we are going to 'improve' Bourne Hill. We mean to make it 50 feet wide everywhere, with proper paved footpaths of Victoria stone or asphalte, and a beautiful roadway of gas tar to match; and as we don't like those curves and bends, we mean to straighten it generally. Those trees are coming down, and even the hawthorns will be out of place in a brand - new Bourne Hill."

The book's back cover - The Pound: The pound was used to imprison stray animals and owners could secure their release by payment to the keeper, or pinder, according to a set scale of charges. If an animal had to be impounded for eight hours or more it had to be fed and watered, and these costs formed part of the payment.

The last pinder was Henry Reed, landlord of "The Woodman," who held the office from 1897 until the pound's closure in December 1904. However it has been preserved. Unfortunately in recent years the pound has become dilapidated, although there are plans for restoration. The postmark on this postcard reads 4th July 1904, when the enclosure was still in use.

"*The Woodman*": The building was originally used for domestic purposes and is postulated to have come into being anytime from 1727 to about a century after! Architectural evidence suggests the more recent end of this span is more likely. Retired police sergeant Henry Wale converted it into the inn we know in 1868 and he remained the landlord until 1893 when Henry Reed, a retired lock maker, and his wife Caroline took over. After Henry's death in 1924 Caroline carried on until her own death in 1948 at the age of 96! The Reeds were the last pinders (keepers) of the nearby Pound, used for impounding stray animals up until 1904.

The front - on shot of the pub is sometime from Henry Reed's time in charge. The other picture views the inn from side on. It's the building with two chimney - stacks in the middle ground.

THE GROVELANDS ESTATE

The next section of pictures includes Grovelands Mansion, Grovelands Park, Winchmore Hill Wood and Broad Walk. A hundred years ago they were all part of the Taylor family's Grovelands Estate. An outline history of these is therefore probably best given under one heading. And a brief outline history is all it is. For more detail please consult Matthew Eccleston's "The Story of Grovelands" and other publications.

At the end of the 16th century the area bounded by Enfield Chase, Church Hill, Hoppers Road and The Bourne/ Bourne Hill (and beyond in places) was covered by the remnants of the ancient Forest of Middlesex. A large tract of this woodland was owned by Lord Burghley. The part now occupied by Grovelands Mansion and Park was known as Lords Grove.

After changing ownership a few times Lords Grove was bought by Walker Gray, a wealthy brandy merchant, in about 1796. He commissioned John Nash (of Brighton Royal Pavilion fame) to build him a new mansion and Humphry Repton to landscape the grounds. The mansion was completed in 1797 and he christened it Southgate Grove.

Gray died in 1834 and the mansion (now called The Grove), with its 260 acres of grounds, were put up for sale without success. The estate passed then into the hands of his relative John Donnithorne Taylor, who at one time held a prominent position in the family business - the famous Taylor Walker brewery. Taylor renamed the house Grovelands. He died in 1885, aged 87, and the estate was inherited by his son Major Robert Kirkpatrick Taylor, who passed away in 1901. This was a big turning point because both J.D. Taylor and his son had employed a private "Green Belt Policy". They were set against urbanisation and had in fact increased the estate to about 317 acres.

In 1902 Major Taylor's son Captain John Vickris Taylor put much of his land in the Palmers Green, Winchmore Hill and Southgate areas up for sale, but only about 2 1/2 acres of the Grovelands Estate were sold.

J.V. Taylor remained at Grovelands until 1908, when he moved to Oxfordshire. The house was vacant until 1916, when he loaned it to the Middlesex Voluntary Aid Detachment for use as a hospital to tend war casualties. Meanwhile in 1911 Southgate Urban District Council purchased 64 acres of the estate and opened it as Grovelands Park two years later, adding further land into the 1930s.

After the sale of the parkland in 1911 the Taylors still owned the remainder of Winchmore Hill Wood, which stood, essentially, to the south east of the park. The Taylors sold this piecemeal to housing developers from about 1912 until 1934. Broad Walk approximates to the line of the old footpath through the Wood.

Returning to the mansion itself, this was sold with the grounds in which it still stands to the Royal Northern Hospital in 1921, and assimilated into the NHS in 1948. It was used as a convalescent home until 1977 when it became vacant and fell into sad decline. The Priory Hospitals Group saved the day in 1985 when they purchased the house and did extensive restoration work. They opened it the following year as Grovelands Priory Hospital for private psychiatric patients. The hospital achieved national fame in 1998 when it temporarily housed General Augusto Pinochet, the former Chilean dictator.

Grovelands Park (right): Another postcard without a date I'm afraid. In the distance the mansion can be seen with the temporary structures so conspicuous in the close up view. In the lake are a number of rowers. I believe this is an activity that died out during the last World War.

Grovelands Hospital (left): This old picture postcard has nothing on its rear to date it. The temporary structures to the south of the mansion have long since gone, but the ha - ha (fence and adjacent ditch) remains today from the era when the Taylors used it to prevent animals from their Deer Park wandering up to their mansion.

Winchmore Hill Wood 1840: I was delighted to come across this old painting by an S. Grosvenor (dated 15th September 1840) in the archives of the "Enfield Gazette," who have kindly given me permission to publish it. I can only presume it is of Wood Cottage, which was the Keeper's Cottage on the path through the wood. Alan Dumayne estimates that the position of the cottage was along Broad Walk opposite Brackendale, where White Timbers stands (to use current day points of reference).

Entrance to the Woods: Thanks to the" Enfield Gazette" for letting me publish this card from their archives. It is postmarked 5th July 1905 and is a view south - west down the footpath, through the Wood, past the Keeper's Cottage close to the entrance to the Wood. (Wood Cottage was about 600 yards down from here, on the right.)

The cottage is recorded in the survey of 1895 but does not appear in the 1865 survey reproduced at page 3 in this book. Its position, were it in existence then, would be just to the left of the tree SW of the "192" printed in the field marked 516.

Broad Walk About 1928 and the photo below it.
Two more of the many pictures the "Enfield Gazette" has been good enough to let me publish.

The 1865 Survey at page 3 shows a row of buildings opposite field 517 at the western end of the Green. These and the Keeper's Cottage at the entrance to the Wood were demolished in the Spring of 1912, so facilitating the construction of Broad Walk along the eastern extremity of the footpath through the wood. Broad Walk is not listed in Kelly's Street Directory until the 1922 edition, although "The Recorder" for 9th December 1915 mentions it. Not until some years after the 1922 listing was full occupancy achieved, whilst the road and pavements were not made up until 1938. Quite an incredible wait when one considers that this is perhaps the wealthiest thoroughfare in the area!

WADES HILL

Reference to the section on Church Hill will reveal that Yarildesfeld was bounded by a lane following the southern course of Wades Hill in the early 13th century. The southern section (still unnamed) is also indicated in the Victoria County History reconstruction of c1600. This shows it running from The Green to terminate (somewhere in the vicinity of where it meets Houndsden Gutter) at Winchmore Hill Gate to Enfield Chase.

Wades Hill is marked on the Edmonton Enclosure Award Map of 1801/2 as Middle Chase Lane. The Victoria County History says it was referred to as Mann's Lane in 1851, though neither the 1838 nor 1845 Directories show a Mann family in residence in the village (Thomas Mann coming to Church Hill in 1858). No name is shown for the lane on the 1865 OS Map, but the 1871 Census portrays it as Kings Head Lane (for obvious reasons). However by the 1881 Census the current name was established.

Regnart's book refers to an account of life in the village in the 1840s and 50s by Harry Cox (born 1839). His father was bailiff to merchant tailor John Wade who lived at Beaumont Lodge on the NW corner of Vicars Moor Lane (see map at page 3). He was reputedly the richest man in the village and allegedly very pompous. It is this gentleman, who died in 1865, who is commemorated in the road's name.

Wades Hill: I am indebted to Mrs U. Collins for this photograph (postmarked April 1904) and permission to publish. There is a full array of shops along the south - east face of Wades Hill. These replaced the beer - garden which had stood opposite the previous incarnation of "The King's Head" until the late 1870s.

Wades Hil: This is an old, but unfortunately undated, picture of the clapperboard cottages at the top of Wades Hill. People are walking north in the middle of a traffic - free road towards Vicars Moor Lane. The cottages date from about 1840 and are shown to the SW corner of field 530 in the 1865 OS Map at page 3. The cottage nearest The Green was occupied by the late Harry Finch, who contributed to "Winchmore Hill Lives."

The Harness Room, Broadfields: Broadfields was built for William Paulin (later Sir William) in the 1870s and so does not appear on the 1865 OS Map. The mansion was near the southern edge of field 537 in that map and was home to William and his wife Fanny, who he married in 1877. She was daughter of Thomas Mann of 'Roseneath', Vicars Moor Lane. The two families achieved national fame with their business relationship in the brewers Mann, Crossman and Paulin.

Lucy Pettifer, nee Maynard, was born in the nearby cottages owned by Paulin in Harwoods Yard in 1901. In "Winchmore Hill Lives," she explained, ".... Paulin Drive of today follows the line of what, in my childhood, was Sir William's private drive from Wades Hill to his beautiful, large, ivy covered mansion. His coaches and horses were kept in the stables where the garage now stands in Wades Hill. The small cottage that remains in Paulin Drive next to the garage was the old harness room. The coachmen were an impressive sight in their top hats."

In 1931, upon the death of Sir William, the 20 acres of Broadfields Estate was auctioned off and turned into housing, excepting the stables and harness room. The latter is shown photographed about 15 years ago in Paulin Drive. It has recently been altered to fit into the new, expensive, Broad Field Court complex of flats.

VICARS MOOR LANE

In the first half of the 13th century Holy Trinity Priory, at Aldgate in the City of London, made a number of purchases in Hegfeld. This field was approximately bounded by what we now call Vicars Moor Lane, Myddleton Gardens, Green Dragon Lane and Hoodcote Gardens. The Victoria County History indicates that the road probably existed as Hagfield Lane in 1349 and was still thus called in c1600.

In 1819 William Robinson wrote of Winchmore Hill, "... it is a large and pleasant village, situated on a considerable eminence. In the lane leading from Bush Hill, near a little thatched cottage, is a well, called 'Vicar's Well,' so called from having been enclosed by a vicar of this parish. It is of antiquity, but what was the vicar's name, and in what year he enclosed it, is not at this day known. The water is very pure, always flowing, and was formerly in great estimation among the inhabitants of the adjacent villages......."

THE COTTAGE, WINCHMORE.

This well would seem to have given its name to the road and it is clearly labelled Vicars Moor Lane on the 1865 OS Map at page 3. Though not shown on page 3, Vicar's Well is indicated on the 1865 Map, but it was closed at a later date after a dead baby's body was found in it. It does not appear on the 1895 OS Map. It was situated about where Pritchett Terrace ends (No 41).

Although the lane long had its "official" title, until about a hundred years ago the villagers often referred to it as "Front Lane." It has a colourful history which can not be covered in this short space.

The illustration of Rose Cottage in the mid 1830s is taken from "Memorials of Thomas Hood" by his daughter Fanny in 1869. L.B Enfield Libraries have kindly given me consent to publish from their copy.

Thomas Hood (1799 - 1845) was a poet and humorist of Scottish descent, who moved to the cottage, often referred to as "Hood's Cottage," from London in 1829. He and his wife were reputed to be of cheerful nature and he was apparently always playing small practical jokes on her, which she took in good spirit. His poem "Our Village" is thought to possibly allude to Winchmore Hill. I heard his "November in England" on the radio recently and thought it fresh enough to have been written yesterday. He seems to have left the area in 1832 after falling out with his landlord over repairs.

Regnart tells us that the cottage was roofed with mossy red - brown shingle tiles. One side of the house had a lawn, beyond which was a vegetable garden. There were also stables and a coach house. I believe it is shown just below the word Moor on the 1865 OS Map at page 3.

"Rose Cottage" was destroyed by the blast from the German V2 rocket that landed in Ringwood Way in November 1944. It was replaced by a new house, whose front bears a blue plaque marking the significance of the site.

The view of the road is postmarked 4th February 1908 and I estimate that it was taken from where the western boundary wall to "Hood's Cottage" now stands, looking towards the railway bridge.

1276. Vicarsmoon Lane, Winchmore Hill.

STATION ROAD

This road must surely have existed as a lane from the village's inception. It is indicated in the Victoria County History's reconstruction of the area c1600 but is unnamed. At one time it was known as Grove Lane, but by the mid 19th century it was called Middle Lane. (Back Lane was Compton Road, Front Lane was Vicars Moor Lane). This is the name clearly shown on the 1865 OS Map at page 3. At that time it was also referred to locally as "Waterses Lane," after the grocer Waters next door to the "Queens Head" where the Delivery Offices now stand.

The railway came in 1871 but the 1895 OS Map still shows Middle Lane, as does the 1899 - 1900 Kelly's Directory. This was changed to Station Road in the 1902 - 3 edition onwards, though it took locals some while to stop using the name Middle Lane.

Middle Lane 1850 - 60: My thanks to the "Enfield Gazette" for permission to publish Miss Ewing's etching, which appears to be based on Dr. Cresswell's sketch near the start of "Memories of a Lost Village." It looks east from the eastern end of the Lower Green, before the railway came, with the boundary to "Roseville" on the right. (From about where 164 is marked on the 1865 OS Map at page 3).

Station Road: This view down Station Road was taken a little further east than Miss Ewing's etching. The card is undated but I would guess it is from about 1930. The house on the left in the middle distance looks as though it may well be the same as the one in her work. If that is the case, then I would tentatively identify it as the premises for Mr and Mrs Binsteds' colourful Bakers and Confectioners described in "Memories of a Lost Village." I believe the building was demolished and replaced by flats in 1973.

Gresley N2 0 - 6 - 2T No 69499 arrives at Winchmore Hill with a train from Kings Cross some time in the 1950s. Thanks to the Gresley Society for permission to publish this snap taken late in the days of steam.

When I came to the area in late 1972 diesel engines were in use on the line, which ran into Kings Cross. I can well remember the tremendous delays in the journey home when the line was being electrified in the tropical Summer of 1976 (when the link was also established between Finsbury Park and the Business hours terminus of Moorgate).

Station Road: This view west up Station Road is undated. In the distance is St. Paul's Institute, which the N13 and N21 Delivery Offices replaced over 30 years ago. The Institute was opened in December 1903 at a cost of about £14,000. It was funded by Sir William Paulin, in memory of his then recently deceased wife Fanny. The January 1908 "Recorder for Palmers Green, Winchmore Hill and Southgate" reports that tree - planting operations were planned for a series of local roads that included Station Road East. This probably puts the photo as being taken anytime from mid 1903 to mid 1908.

FORDS GROVE

I am grateful to the Everett sisters for letting me have this postcard of Fords Grove and agreeing to its publication.

According to an "Enfield Gazette" article in 1925 the lane probably obtained its name from a family named Forde, which was settled in the area in the middle of the 13th century. I have come across a paper from the 1530s referring to Fords Green, in the vicinity, so this may well be so.

The Victoria County History map for the area c1600 shows the lane as being called New Lane. In the 1861 Census it is referred to as Grove Lane and Miss Cresswell describes it when out with her father, the village doctor, around this time.

"All walks with the Doctor were pleasant, and the oaks and elms made the lane green and shady. In the wide ditches were sticklebacks and frogspawn and wonderful caddis - worms, housed in tiny pieces of stick or collections of little gravel stones. Water rats splashed and swam under the banks, and in places the mud was painted scarlet with masses of threadworms.... It was a favourite stroll for lovers and old folks in the summer evenings, and they mostly sat upon the logs to rest, and listen to the nightingales who sang rapturously in the snow - white hawthorns."

The lane is unnamed on the 1865 OS Map, but is marked as Middle Lane on the 1895 revision. By this time the villagers were calling it "Mortiboy's Lane," after the farmer at Fords Grove Farm. Edward Mortiboy is shown in residence there in the 1899 - 1900 Kelly's Street Directory, where the name Fords Grove is used. Only three other residents are shown for the lane.

The Enfield Gazette of 31st October 1924 reports that, "More than half the southern side of Fords Grove has been recently covered with houses; the road is being widened and a footway constructed."

Mortiboy's Farm: My thanks to Mr J. Waring for supplying this undated photo' with permission to publish.

The farmhouse shown was on the south side of Fords Grove about 200 yards down from Green Lanes. It was thought to date from the early 17th century and in the mid 19th century was occupied by the Tills family. Captain Tills, who died in the early 1860s, served at the Battle of Trafalgar. His only son Frank joined the Army as a Private and was killed in India, after being promoted to an NCO. Miss Cresswell described the cottage of this era as having, "diamond - paned leaded windows and (a) mossy roof of shingle tiles, every shade of rich red and brown, bright near the eaves with yellow patches of poor - man's - pepper, light green mosses and huge rosettes of house - leeks."

In 1871 the Tills left and the Mortiboys started a forty year tenancy. They rented land on both sides of Fords Grove from the Busk family, who for many years resided at Fords Grove Mansion (where Capitol House now sits). The Mortiboys supplied the villagers with their milk and were such a feature of local life that the farm was called "Mortiboy's Farm" and the road "Mortiboy's Lane."

By 1911 the farmhouse floors and roof had deteriorated to such an extent that Southgate Council issued a closing order on it. It thereafter became an ivy - covered ruin before being demolished. However, the foundations were still visible in the early 1920s and in September 1925 the "Enfield Gazette" when visiting the site noted, "the old farm well still exists and despite the drought it contained plenty of water."

A 1933 "Gazette" article refers to the Cottage as having occupied the sites of 14 - 20 Fords Grove.

HOPPERS ROAD

The Victoria County History reconstruction for c1600 shows Hoppers Road existing along its current line, though it is unnamed. The Edmonton Enclosure Award 1801/2 refers to it as Hoppers Lane, as does 'The Grove' (Grovelands) sale catalogue of 1834. However, it is marked as Hoppers Road on the 1865 OS Map and the name remained unchanged thereafter.

Salisbury Cottages, Hoppers Road: This photograph was kindly given, with agreement to publication, by Mrs Gwen Webb. Her grandfather was Henry 'Tiddles' Hemington and one of his brothers, Alfred Walter 'Spurgeon,' is pictured driving Aldridge's cart in the Ice Wells picture in "Winchmore Hill Lives." One of their brothers was William 'Rat' who achieved local fame for his abilities as a runner. He lived for many years at Salisbury Cottages, where he raised a large family.

Mrs Webb believes the picture might have been taken on June 22nd 1911 when George V was crowned king. At that time the old 'Salisbury Arms' stood further north on the road and the site of the current (larger) inn was occupied by Salisbury Cottages and the mansion of Belmont House.

This section of road was redeveloped in a form more like its present one in the mid 1930s.

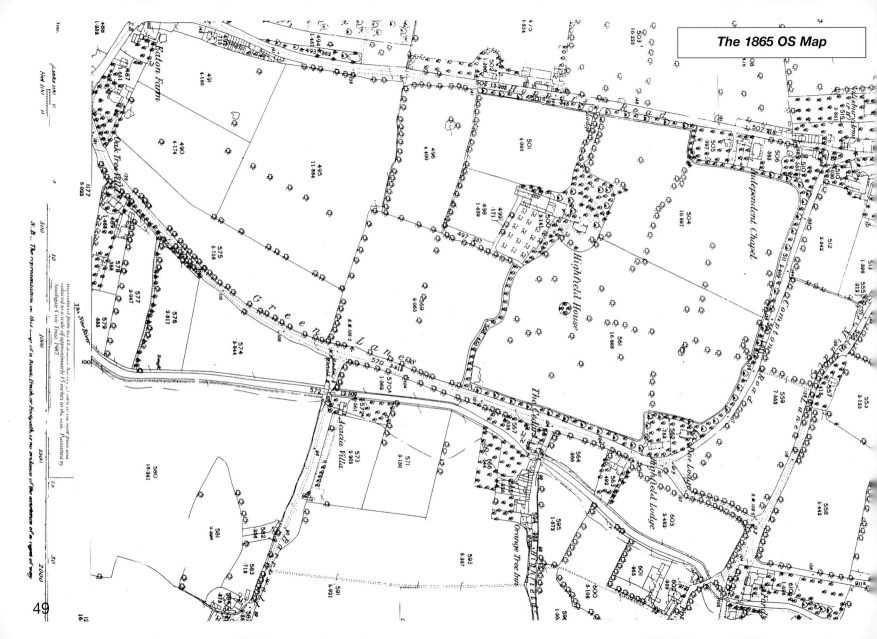

The 1865 OS Map

49

Highfield Park: I am grateful to the Ordnance Survey and Southgate Civic Trust for permission to publish the extract from the 1865 Survey (not reproduced to scale). The reader will see that Highfield House is shown set in the extensive estate of Highfield Park, which was bounded by Hoppers Road, Compton Road, Green Lanes and about what is now Woodberry Avenue. My thanks to Mrs Nancy Hicks, nee Andrew, for giving me the results of her research and her personal recollections on the area, which have contributed significantly to the following.

The House was probably built c1815 with its main access being from Hoppers Road via a tree - lined pathway that approximated to the line of Arundel Gardens. Little is known of the House until the 1841 Census shows it as being in the hands of the Frith family. The 1851 and 1861 returns indicate Elizabeth Clark from Wiltshire as Head of Household.

1861 was in Henrietta Cresswell's childhood and she wrote, " Highfield Park was for many years (the children's) free playground. There were two large meadows, known as the upper ten - acre and the lower ten - acre, separated by a fence of iron hurdles.... The soft 'whoo - whoo,' of the white owls and the hissing of the baby owls in the nest, the rustling of small things in the grass, the grunt of a hedgehog, the nibbling of the sheep and the baaing of lambs in the upper ten - acre, the stamp of a horse's hoof as he shook off the gnats by the pond, the white mist wreaths rising from the grass...."

1871 saw the railway bite a fragment from the NW corner of the estate. That year's Census shows George Bartlett from Wiltshire as Head of Household. Ten years on the Census indicates Thomas Kelsey had replaced him. It was he who gave the land upon which the Methodist Churches were built.

Little more is known of the house until 1895, when Mr Wilkinson bought it, and it stayed in his family's hands until 1947. In his "The Cresswells of Winchmore Hill" Peter Hodge states that on 5th April 1894, further to involvement by Henrietta's brother Francis, St. Bartholomews Hospital bought 10 acres of land opposite Highfield Road for sports fields from the executors of the late Alfred Walker, of Stone Hall fame. The grounds, including pavilion, were opened in June 1895.

This transaction reminds us how little is known of ownership prior to 1895 despite details of occupancy. The Edmonton Enclosure Award of 1801/2 indicates that the estate was then in plots held by at least four different owners. We do not know how these plots were amalgamated, when and by whom.

The 1895 OS Map shows the estate essentially unchanged since the 1865 survey, excepting marginal transgression by the railway and the new sports ground. However, the 1899 - 1900 Kelly's Street Directory, which shows Samuel Wilkinson occupying Highfield House, lists Fernleigh Road (though without occupants). By the outbreak of the Great War, most of the old Park (other than the Sports Ground) was the housing we know today. The undated aerial photograph shows much of this. St. Paul's Institute in Station Road is in the distance at the centre, with the open ground of Roseneath Estate opposite, suggesting a pre 1932 origin.

Compton & Haslemere Rds.Winchmore Hill.from the Air.　1456

51

The other picture, also undated, was given to me by Gordon Farrant, Director of Putts Estate Agents in Grange Park. He has also kindly consented to publication.

The mansion remained with the Wilkinsons after the sale of surrounding land and they improved it. However, from about 1922 the house was rented by a Miss Chislett, who opened Winchmore Hill High School in it, the entrance being in Arundel Gardens. In 1933 the ten - year old Nancy moved to that street and attended the school. She says, "The grounds contained three tennis courts, a playground, stables, a cottage and gardens full of bushes and trees. The school's gymnasium was in the House's old ballroom and the 4th Form was housed in what had once been the Billiards Room. The school closed in 1939 on the outbreak of war and the buildings were used as an Auxiliary Fire Station ; the garden front of the house was then concreted over for parking the fire engines."

The Wilkinsons sold the house to Southgate Council in 1947, but it remained empty and dilapidated until demolished in 1951.

In 1954 the Council erected flats and Mrs Hicks tells us that the large cedar tree that remains in their grounds was once a favourite meeting place for the schoolgirls of her era.

Old Hoppers Road, Winchmore Hill: This photograph, dated c1890, is reproduced by kind permission of LB Enfield Libraries.

The current premises for the 'Dog and Duck' date from 1900 and this snap shows its predecessor in a row of similar looking cottages. Two of these (Nos 80 and 82 Hoppers Road) remain today and are thought to have been built about 1770. Perhaps the old inn dated from the same era. It gave its name to Dog and Duck Lane, now known as Bourne Hill.

Eaton Farm in 1860 from a water - colour sketch by the late Dr. John Cresswell.

I am indebted to the "Enfield Gazette" for this gem from its archives.

In "Memories of a Lost Village" Miss Cresswell describes the Little Wonder bus journey from London in the middle of the nineteenth century,

".... The 'bus then turned westward along Silver Street (which) led to the 'Highlands' of Winchmore Hill and Southgate..... On the right, as Hoppers Road was entered, stood a row of cottages with long gardens. Next to them was Eaton Farm with old barns roofed with antique mossy tiles. At the turning by the 'Dog and Duck' Southgate passengers alighted....."

The cottages stood on the road opposite St. John's Church of today and some of them were replaced by Eaton Villa and its adjoining stables, now a garage. Then coming north west to the bend of Hoppers Road was Eaton Farmhouse, which is believed to have been pulled down about 1870.

This view looks back down from the bend in Hoppers Road towards Green Lanes with the railings to a pond, that occupied

much of the roadway, in the lower left hand corner. The trees past the farmhouse stand where today's garage is. There was also a fair sized pond in the farmyard and a well with windlass.

Eaton Farm got its name from William Eaton, who owned the plot of land in 1800. He also then owned land in Edmonton and to the NW of what is now Winchmore Hill Road. Under the Edmonton Enclosure Award 1801/2 he bought further plots near the Farm. The Eaton Villa and Eaton Park Road of today clearly get their name from their proximity to land formerly held by William Eaton.

GREEN LANES

The Victoria County History reconstruction for c1600 shows that this lane probably existed by then but was not yet called Green Lanes. The part just south of The Broadway of today was then called Highfield Lane.

In the paper "Drovers and Tanners of Enfield and Edmonton," J. Burnby suggests that the long and extensive lane was once used by drovers bringing cattle to London markets from distant parts of Britain. Possibly from about 1750 the cattle were sold in Barnet rather than more centrally, whence Green Lanes in Winchmore Hill would no longer have been a cattle trail. The paper suggests that the relatively high number of Welsh derived names in the Enfield and Edmonton areas could be explained by the proposed association with the Welsh cattle trade. (The Udall family, so influential in Winchmore Hill in the 19th century, was said to be of Welsh extraction).

The 1865 OS Map shows Green Lanes thus marked and it has remained so ever since.

"The Green Dragon" - The Victoria County History says that a "Green Dragon" inn had been established by 1750. It was originally on the eastern side of Green Lanes, opposite Green Dragon Lane i.e what we call Mason's Corner. In the late 18th century it seems some murderers were caught near the inn and hung on gallows erected nearby. These were not pulled down for many months, so motivating the landlord to move to the present site about 1800. This second inn was replaced by the current structure in 1893.

Much has been written about the 'Green Dragon' but surely one of the best pieces must be this extract from a 1925 "Enfield Gazette" article.

"The old 'Green Dragon' was a low white building with pillared portico, with an overhead bracket lamp. For many years it was known as a very sporty house, and, like its successor 25 years ago, it was on Sundays and on summer evenings the first house of call, and frequently the destination before return home, of the trotting horse fanciers from London, who would drive out in their sulkies and buggies, timing themselves from known distances. Every conceivable kind of horse - drawn vehicle was to be seen either in the gravelled yard or drawn up at the roadside.

1279. The Rookery, Winchmore Hill.

In the days of cock - fighting and prize - fighting, the old 'Green Dragon' was a favourite resort of the 'fancy', and many encounters attracted large numbers of spectators. Some sixty years ago, the landlord was a Scot named William Macdonald, who was a noted breeder of and dealer in dogs. His Italian greyhounds, toy bull - terriers and pugs were famous all over the country. His sale of a pug to the Marquis of Huntly created a record price in its day, the £40 being then regarded as quite sensational. There were large kennels at the rear of the inn, in which were housed very fine specimens of all the then popular breeds, which besides being in themselves a profitable business, attracted much custom to the inn.

This old inn was at one time the virtual post office of the village, for in the 'forties of the last century the bright yellow mail coach carried postal matter to the 'Green Dragon' once a day, and there residents had to call for their letters. It was also the home of the 'Little Wonder' bus which cut the return fare to London down from five shillings to half - a - crown - and today we find history repeating itself, for the 'Green Dragon' is the terminus of the 'Admirals', rapidly travelling motor 'buses each having seating accommodation for 46 passengers and leading the way in the reduction of fares."

The first photograph is from a card postmarked 21st August 1920. To the viewer's right are the stables which remain today in the premises of Ironside Motors. In November 2000 Mr. Ironside was good enough to give me a quick tour of these. The old hayloft is nowadays used for car parts, whilst the pigeon loft remains vacant.

The other (undated) picture is a winter view of the inn from the gardens of "Beaulieu." These lovely gardens were noted locally for their birds.

August 10th, 1811: His Majesty's Postmaster - General

I am indebted to the Post Office Heritage collections for agreement to publish this old notice.

In 1680 William Dockwra set up an illegal rival to the state system with his Penny Post, whereby he undertook to convey letters and small packets for 1d within about a seven mile radius of Central London. This was so successful that in 1682 it was assimilated into the Crown System. In 1801 the Penny Post became the Two Penny Post and this poster announces a change to circulation whereby a letter posted in Southgate for Winchmore Hill, say, would go direct rather than via a central hub.

It seems Gibraltar Cottages, on the corner of Firs Lane and Green Lanes, may at one time have served in the postal system. We know that Pigot and Co's 'London Directory' for 1826 contains an entry for "Southgate and Winchmore Hill (Middlesex)" that includes "Post Office, Winchmore Hill, receiving house at Wm. Board's the 'Green Dragon', from whence letters are dispatched at half past eight morning and at half past three afternoon."

In 1840 the world's first uniform national tariff was introduced along with the Penny Black stamp. In 1904 a sorting office was built opposite St. Paul's Institute on the corner of Kings Avenue/Station Road. That building remains today, but in private use because The Royal Mail moved to its existing premises in about 1970, after the demise of the Institute. Both the N13 and N21 deliveries are handled from here. Postal staff say that the building is haunted!

August 10*th*, 1811.

HIS MAJESTY'S POSTMASTER-GENERAL

Being desirous of extending the Benefit and Accommodation afforded to the Public by Means of the Two-penny Post-Office, have been pleased to order that on and after the above date, Letters passing from one to another of the following Places : viz.

Kingsland	Clapton	Winchmore Hill
Ball's Pond	Stoke Newington	Enfield
Dalston	Stamford Hill	Bull's Cross
Shacklewell	Tottenham	Ponder's End,
Hackney	Edmonton	and
Homerton	Southgate	Enfield Highway.

or from one Part to another of either of the same Places, be delivered direct, by Means of a Bye-Post, instead of being first sent to London.

By this Regulation, Letters put in at these Places in time for the Morning Dispatch are delivered at any of them about Noon, and such as are put in for the Afternoon Dispatch, the same Evening; Thus the Letters are delivered shortly after they are put into the Post, and Answers can be received a Day earlier than they could previous to this arrangement.

In order that Persons receiving Letters may know whether they have passed duly through the Post-Office, and whether they are delivered in proper time, every Unpaid Letter has a stamped figure of 3 denoting the Postage to be paid a Delivery, and every Paid Letter a Stamp shewing that it is Post Paid and where it was put in. Each Letter, Paid or Unpaid, has also a Stamp which shews the Place it was dispatched from, and the Day and time of Day that is Mg. for Morning and Ev. for Evening) of its departure. The following are the Forms of these Stamps.

On the front of each Unpaid Letter.	On the front of each Post Paid Letter, according to where put in.	One of these on the back of each Letter, according to where dispatched from &c.
3	Tottenham 3 Py P Paid	

This Bye Post to be considered an Experiment only, until further Notice.

E. JOHNSON, Comptroller.

ILLEGAL CONVEYANCE OF LETTERS.

By the 9th of Queen Anne, cap. 10. Any Person illegally conveying Letters, incurs a Penalty of £5 for every offence, and £100 for every Week the Practice is continued. And by 42d. Geo. III. cap. 81. the Sender also incurs a penalty of £5 for every Offence with full Costs of Suit.

Beaulieu: My thanks to L.B Enfield Libraries for allowing publication of this shot from their archives.

The mansion, situated near today's Beaulieu Gardens, dated from the 18th century and at the start of the 19th century it and its ten acres of grounds were in the hands of John Gray, brother of Walker who built the mansion we now call Grovelands. William Cass bought the property for £4,750 in 1806 and his family retained it until 1832. Sometime between 1823 and the Cass's departure John Papworth laid out the grounds, which occupied the area bounded by Green Lanes, Firs Lane and The New River, with a southern boundary just below Elm Park Road's lower end.

The grounds boasted a great diversity of trees, which supported an equally varied population of birds and other wildlife. The Paulin family occupied Beaulieu for eight years from 1865. However, the construction of Elm Park Road in 1898/9 heralded the beginning of the end. The glory of Beaulieu faded and it became a rather sad ruin before its demolition in 1937.

Century House: This dignified building was erected by the Rowley Brothers firm of builders. It was their hundredth house and was occupied by family members until 1971, when the local Conservatives took it over. Enfield Southgate was at that time a very safe Tory seat. In 1984 MP Sir Anthony Berry was tragically killed by the IRA's Brighton bomb blast and was succeeded by "Golden Boy" Michael Portillo, tipped by many to succeed John Major as Tory leader. However, in the lead up to the 1997 General Election the Conservatives' intended sale of Century House made the national press, owing to the strong local opposition at plans to sell to a fast food outlet. Some people consider this a contributing factor to Mr Portillo's demise in Labour's landslide win of 1997, so ruling him out of the ensuing race to lead the Opposition.

This picture was taken in July 1999, but Century House has since been demolished and will give way to flats.

The Broadway: The Victoria County History's reconstruction for c1600 shows the Broadway area as Fords Green. The name probably derives from a Forde family who lived in the vicinity in the middle of the 13th century. I have seen a document in the Guildhall Library from the 1530s that refers to an agreement between two farmers at Fords Green.

No separate or distinctive name for this part of Green Lanes is indicated in the 1865 or 1895 Surveys. Regnart tells us that in the late 19th century, "What is now the Broadway had fields on either side with trees meeting overhead."

The two cards show adjacent views of the SW corner of the Broadway. The one with the horse - drawn vehicles bears a postmark of Ju 18th 1909. The west side of the Broadway is shown for the first time in the Kelly's Street Directories in the 1904 - 5 edition, boasting a full range of shops. (The east side is first indicated in the 1910 - 11 edition, with just two businesses).

THE BROADWAY, WINCHMORE HILL N.

Eaton Park Wesleyan Chapel 1880: I am grateful to Rev. Sheehan of Winchmore Hill Methodist Church for allowing me to use this drawing and former steward D.J. Swinson for his photos and information. This caption is largely based on that information and R.F. Farrant's "A History of the Winchmore Hill Methodist Church 1880 - 1980."

There are records that the Rev. John Rattenbury of the Hackney Circuit occasionally preached in a small hall in Hoppers Road as far back as 1850, but nothing regular evolved. However, a few years later Thomas Kelsey moved from Stamford Hill to Highfield House in Hoppers Road. He built extensively in Bowes Park and the nearby Eaton Park Estate. 1n 1879 he offered a site on the edge of that estate to the Finsbury Park Wesleyan Methodist Circuit, on condition that they build a chapel on it and hold regular services.

Apparently this offer was received with some caution, owing to the comparatively low population in such a rural area. However, the Rev. Peter Thompson (Minister at Wood Green) accepted and he and William Kilner became joint treasurers for the fund raising.

The stone laying of the original chapel took place on 30th November 1880 and that evening it was announced the building would cost £1,200, of which £800 was already to hand. Unfortunately the fears about the low rural population seemed founded in the early years and congregations were meagre, unless supplemented from surrounding areas. However, in Edwardian times with the coming of the tram, and the nearby housing developments, the situation improved greatly. This prompted calls for a new church.

Tenders were invited and the cheapest of £5,086 was selected. The new church was built in front of the old Chapel and was opened on 28th September 1912 with seating for 750. The Chapel illustrated became the Church Hall and, in 1932, a small hall was added to its rear.

By the 1980s the Church, like most others nationally, was suffering a decline in attendances whilst the cost of maintaining such a large building was excessive. So it was that on 10th April 1987 the current smaller church was opened. Part of the 1880 Chapel remains as the Church Hall.

St. Monica's Catholic Church: This is an undated postcard from a Stonard Road perspective, rather than the more familiar Green Lanes one.

The booklet, "Seventy Five Years of Saint Monica's Palmers Green 1910 - 1985" tells us that the Catholic parish of Palmers Green was established in 1910 when a private house was hired in Grovelands Road to say mass. In 1911 the service moved north to a house opposite St. John's Church in Green Lanes (now a parade of shops). In 1912 Fr. Patrick Gallagher was appointed rector. It seems he was a man of immense drive and energy with business experience as a builder. Under his guidance the current church's grounds were purchased. The church, with accommodation for over 400, was opened on 4th May 1914 by Cardinal Bourne. The land, church and presbytery together cost £6,600. The Parish Hall, later to achieve fame as The Intimate Theatre, was not added until 1931.

The parish was probably dedicated to St. Monica at Fr. Gallagher's suggestion and is one of only two in the Westminster Diocese to be so. She was born in 332 AD at Tagaste in North Africa and married Patricius, a pagan from the same town, whom she helped convert to Christianity. They had three children, the eldest of whom became St. Augustine. She died at Ostia near Rome in 387 AD and is regarded by the church as a special patroness of married women and widows.

Perhaps it is fitting that at the church opening two suffragettes stationed themselves at the entrance gates distributing leaflets. They appealed to a church dignitary to, "pray for the women, my Lord."

The Ghost of J.D. Taylor

The air hangs still
Over Winchmore Hill
As darkness falls to ground
And on The Green
There's faintly seen
A man in Victorian gown

Each Sunday night
He's a familiar sight
For those who come this way
And as he nears
Well tuned ears
Hear what he has to say

"I can't believe
I can't conceive
The damage that's been done
Those country lanes
For years the same
Yet now I can't find one

I kept my land
You'll understand
To keep the village green
It's such a shame
'Twas all in vain
To me it seems obscene"

The morning lark
In Grovelands Park
Heralds in the dawn
The ghost has gone
With the blackbird's song
As the mist clears from the lawn

Our Winchmore Hill
Is lovely still
A suburb of London with charm
But JD's surely right
A better sight
Was the village amongst wood and farm